In City Gardens

Written and Photographed by George Ancona

📖 CelebrationPress

An Imprint of ScottForesman
A Division of HarperCollinsPublishers

Flowers, vegetables, and fruit are growing all over our city.

It all begins when our neighbors decide to get together and grow a garden for the neighborhood. We clean up an empty lot, field, or playground. First we clear out the junk, dig up the dirt, and take out the rocks.

Then we add lots of rich, dark compost to make the earth healthy for our plants and seeds.

Then we plant seeds
in rows, which some
day will grow into
flowers and vegetables.

Around the fences of the gardens and
playgrounds, we dig holes and plant shrubs
and trees that grow tall and wide to shade
us from the hot summer sun.

Every day we water the garden
so that the thirsty plants
will have lots to drink.

And every day they get a little taller and wider.

Weeds also grow in the gardens around
our plants and flowers.

We use hoes and shovels to get rid of the hungry weeds that gobble up the water and energy that our plants need.

We put the weeds into a compost bin along with twigs, grass cuttings, straw, manure, and vegetable and fruit trimmings.

This makes a nice home for busy worms that turn all that organic stuff into compost. When compost is added to the garden it holds the water and gives the plants the nutrients they need to grow.

How to Make Compost

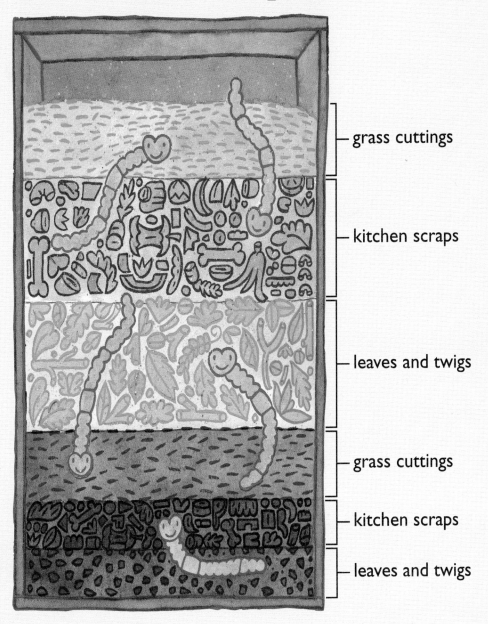

grass cuttings

kitchen scraps

leaves and twigs

grass cuttings

kitchen scraps

leaves and twigs

While the city traffic roars by, the plants in the gardens are slowly getting taller, spreading their leaves and opening their flowers. Among the leaves we find beans, tomatoes, squash, peas, corn, and many other vegetables. The branches sag under the weight of the apples, peaches, and pears.

It's harvest time. Now it's time to pick the vegetables, flowers, and fruit that we planted in the spring.

And, of course,
the best part
is when we get
to taste and eat
all the good
food that we
have grown.